The Weather of the Heart

poems by
Madeleine L'Engle

Harold Shaw Publishers
Wheaton, Illinois

Grateful acknowledgment is made:

To Seabury Press, New York, for the use of poems which first appeared in The Irrational Season, © *1977.*

To Farrar, Straus & Giroux, Inc., New York, for the use of poems which first appeared in Lines Scribbled on an Envelope, © *1969.*

ISBN 0-87788-931-7

Cover photo: Gary Irving

Library of Congress Catalog Card Number: 78-62202

1st Printing, cloth edition, August 1978
2nd Printing, cloth edition, September 1981
1st Printing, paper edition, April 1987
2nd Printing, paper edition, August 1988
3rd Printing, paper edition, March 1990
4th Printing, paper edition, September 1990
5th Printing, paper edition, August 1991

for Harold and Luci

Contents

Introduction   7
Within This Strange and Quickened Dust   9
To a Long Loved Love: 1   10
To a Long Loved Love: 2   11
To a Long Loved Love: 3   12
To a Long Loved Love: 4   13
To a Long Loved Love: 5   14
To a Long Loved Love: 6   15
To a Long Loved Love: 7   16
Epiphany   17
Lovers Apart   18
Lines after Sir Thomas Browne   20
Lines after Herbert: Rondel   21
Epidaurus: the Theatre: an Actor Muses   22
The Mermaid   23
The Parrot   24
The Animals Do Judge   25
Burn, Charity   26
Shout Joy!   28
The Guests of Abraham   30
Jacob: Ballade   31
Moses   32
David   34
Song from the Fiery Furnace   36
From St. Luke's Hospital (1)   37
From St. Luke's Hospital (2)   38
From St. Luke's Hospital (3)   39
Abraham's Child   40
Tree at Christmas   42
Annunciation   44
After Annunciation   45
Like Every Newborn   46
The Risk of Birth   47
The Winter Is Cold, Is Cold   48
Fire by Fire   49
Act III, Scene ii   50
The Sea Bishop   51
The Dragon   52
The Phoenix   54
The Sea Monster   56

Instruments   *58*
Body, the Black Horse and the White   *59*
Word   *60*
. . . Set to the Music of the Spheres   *61*
For M. S. J. 20th June, 1968   *62*
For Dana: 4th November   *63*
Charlotte Rebecca Jones, 22nd August, 1969   *64*
Charlotte   *65*
Epithalamion   *66*
Crosswicks   *67*
O Sapientia   *68*
O Simplicitas   *69*
God's Beast   *71*
The Tenth Hour   *72*
Pentecost   *74*
Corinth   *75*
Ready for Silence   *76*
Advent, 1971   *77*
Come, Lord Jesus!   *78*
Come, Let Us Gather   *79*
At Communion   *80*
Martha   *81*
Temper My Intemperance   *82*
Sonnet After Thomas   *83*
Love Letter   *84*
For Ascension Day   *86*
After the Saturday Liturgy at Montfort   *88*
Star Light   *90*
Ascension, 1969   *92*
Confession Shortly Before the Forty-eighth Birthday   *93*
Testament   *94*
Sonnet, Trinity 18   *96*

FORE WORD

Poetry and prayer are synonymous in my life, and because both are a gift, which I accept with joy and sometimes pain, I seldom know whether I have served the gift well or ill. But perhaps that doesn't really matter; the important thing is to be willing–to want to serve the gift whenever it comes, either as verse or prayer.

Usually it teaches me something–something about God and therefore something about myself–because I have come to realize that my search for God and my search for me are one and the same. Or, rather, when I search my own heart, God shows me his instead; and in my search for him I find myself.

Sometimes I send these searchings and findings across the country to friends in letters, and receive from them their searchings and findings in return, and I have learned that to share poetry is one of the most intimate acts of friendship possible–and one that makes us the most vulnerable. But if we refuse to take that risk we are less than alive.

My heart's climate is not constant; I doubt if anyone's is. My inner weather shifts with the days. But much sunshine has shone on me through the sharing and giving and receiving.

And so I am taught to pray. And so I am taught to be.

—Madeleine L'Engle
"Crosswicks" June 1978

Within This Strange
and Quickened Dust

O God, within this strange and quickened dust
The beating heart controls the coursing blood
In discipline that holds in check the flood
But cannot stem corrosion and dark rust.
In flesh's solitude I count it blest
That only you, my Lord, can see my heart
With passion's darkness tearing it apart
With storms of self, and tempests of unrest.
But your love breaks through blackness, bursts with light;
We separate ourselves, but you rebind
In Dayspring all our fragments; body, mind,
And spirit join, unite against the night.
Healed by your love, corruption and decay
Are turned, and whole, we greet the light of day.

To a Long Loved Love: 1

We, who have seen the new moon grow old together,
Who have seen winter rime the fields and stones
As though it would claim earth and water forever,
We who have known the touch of flesh and the shape of
    bones
Know the old moon stretching its shadows across a
    whitened field
More beautiful than spring with all its spate of blooms;
What passion knowledge of tried flesh still yields,
What joy and comfort these familiar rooms.

To a Long Loved Love: 2

In the moonless, lampless dark now of this bed
My body knows each line and curve of yours;
My fingers know the shape of limb and head:
As pure as mathematics ecstasy endures.
Blinded by night and love we share our passion,
Certain of burning flesh, of living bone:
So feels the sculptor in the moment of creation
Moving his hands across the uncut stone.

11

To a Long Loved Love: 3

I know why a star gives light
Shining quietly in the night;
Arithmetic helps me unravel
The hours and years this light must travel
To penetrate our atmosphere.
I count the craters on the moon
With telescopes to make them clear.
With delicate instruments I measure
Secrets of barometric pressure.

Therefore I find it inexpressibly queer
That with my own soul I am out of tune,
That I have not stumbled on the art
Of forecasting the weather of the heart.

To a Long Loved Love: 4

You are still new, my love. I do not know you,
Stranger beside me in the dark of bed,
Dreaming the dreams I cannot ever enter,
Eyes closed in that unknown, familiar head.
Who are you, who have thrust and entered
My very being, penetrated so that now
I can never again be wholly separate,
Bound by shared living to this unknown thou?
I do not know you, nor do you know me,
And yet we know each other in the way
Of our primordial forbears in the garden,
Adam knew Eve. As we do, so did they.
They, we, forever strangers: Austere but true.
And yet I would not change it. You are still new.

To a Long Loved Love: 5

Words must be said, and silences be kept,
Yet, that word better left unheard, unspoken,
Like that unsaid, can wound. O Love, I've wept
From words, have thought my heart was broken
From the looked-for word unuttered. Where
Silence should speak loud, we speak instead.
Where words of love would heal we do not dare
To voice them: From sound and silence both have fled.
Yet love grows through those quiet deepening hours
When silence fills the empty boundless spaces
Twixt flesh and flesh. Wordlessness is ours
And love is nourished through unspoken graces.
But O my love, as I need daily bread
I need the words of love which must be said.

To a Long Loved Love: 6

Neither sadist nor masochist, I still
Must turn to violence: break, be broken.
False image of myself I beg you: kill.
Help me destroy the one of you I've spoken
Within my wilful heart. It is no more you
Than I am all that I would wish to be.
I cannot really love you till I hew
All these projections of an unreal me,
An imaged you, to shards. Then death
Will have a chance to free me for creation.
God! All this dying has me out of breath.
How do I understand reincarnation?
But if I burst all bonds of self-protection
Then may I find us both in resurrection.

To a Long Loved Love: 7

Because you're not what I would have you be
I blind myself to who, in truth, you are.
Seeking mirage where desert blooms, I mar
Your *you*. Aaah, I would like to see
Past all delusion to reality:
Then would I see God's image in your face,
His hand in yours, and in your eyes his grace.
Because I'm not what I would have me be,
I idolize Two who are not any place,
Not you, not me, and so we never touch.
Reality would burn. I do not like it much.
And yet in you, in me, I find a trace
Of love which struggles to break through
The hidden lovely truth of me, of you.

Epiphany

Unclench your fists
Hold out your hands.
Take mine.
Let us hold each other.
Thus is his Glory
Manifest.

Lovers Apart

In what, love, does fidelity consist?
I will be true to you, of course.
My body's needs I can resist,
Come back to you without remorse;

And you, behind the footlight's lure,
Kissing an actress on the stage,
Will leave her presence there, I'm sure,
As I my people on the page.

And yet—I love you, darling, yet
I sat with someone at a table
And gloried in our minds that met
As sometimes strangers' minds are able

To leap the bounds of times and spaces
And find, in sharing wine and bread
And light in one another's faces
And in the words that each has said

An intercourse so intimate
It shook me deeply, to the core.
I said good-night, for it was late;
We parted at my hotel door

And I went in, turned down the bed
And took my bath and thought of you
Leaving the theatre with light tread
And going off, as you should do,

To rest, relax, and eat and talk—
And I lie there and wonder who
Will wander with you as you walk
And what you both will say and do . . .

We may not love in emptiness;
We married in a peopled place;
The vows we made enrich and bless
The smile on every stranger's face,

And all the years that we have spent
Give me the joy that makes me able
To love and laugh with sacrament
Across a strange and distant table.

No matter where I am, you are,
We two are one and bread is broken
And laughter shared both near and far
Deepens the promises once spoken

And strengthens our fidelity
Although I cannot tell you how,
But I rejoice in mystery
And rest upon our marriage vow.

Lines after Sir Thomas Browne

If thou couldst empty self of selfishness
And then with love reach out in wide embrace
Then might God come this purer self to bless;
So might thou feel the wisdom of His Grace,
And see, thereby, the radiance of His face.

But selfishness turns inwards, miry, black,
Refuses stars, sees only clouded night,
Too full, too dark, cannot confess a lack,
Turns from God's face, blest, holy, bright,
Is blinded by the presence of the Light.

Lines after Herbert: Rondel

The contrarieties crush me. These crosse actions
Do winde a rope about, and cut my heart.
Good deeds are turned to sudden malefactions.
The end was never guessed at in the start.

How these stern contradictions break apart
The simplest words, and purest actions.
The contrarieties crush me: these crosse factions
Do winde a rope about and cut my heart.

A fearsome faith provides the only cautions.
O dear my Father, ease my smart.
Reality permits of no abstractions.
The whole is visioned in each broken part.
The contrarieties crush me: the crosse's actions
Do winde a rope about and hold my heart.

21

Epidaurus: the Theatre: an Actor Muses

Truth is always masked,
is revealed, for mortals, only in signs.
With these magnificent flawed words
I reach for those harsh verities
which are past all the eager crowd
is willing to endure, truth being
neither charitable nor kind.
Behind the mask my face is distorted
by the dispassionate power
of the stern events I act, brutality of man,
inevitable punishment of fate
set in motion by the unconcerned
justice of the gods
who, being immortal,
are nonetheless concerned
with mortality,
dabble in it, consort with it,
to our destruction
and—perhaps—their shame.
with action and with words I reach
beyond the gods for that transcendent truth
which must, for us, be masked
or strike us dead.

The Mermaid

My father gives me everything
I ask for. Don't you envy me?
I can swim faster than a bird can wing.
Sea gulls cannot catch me: see?
Who else has hair of silk sea green?
Or silver scales, shining, alive?
My father's king (there is no queen).
I can dive full fathom five.

You wonder why I never cry?
Why mermaids have no need for tears?
Upon my sea-salt rock I lie
And play with time and laugh at years
And send my song along the air
And sing my call to passing ships,
And there is nothing quite so fair
As the cold touch of dead men's lips.

My father gives me everything,
Gold and frankincense and mer-
Boys for my sport. I lie and sing.
A sailor shouts, "Don't look at her!"
I lie upon my sea-swept stone
And wait. The sailor hears and cries.
More bleached white bones to call my own.
And his salt tears before he dies.

My father gives me everything.

That's just sea water in my eyes.

The Parrot

It was better in the jungle.
There I could imitate
the sound of dawn.
I could speak with the voice
of many tongues
and even if I didn't understand
I was still, in a sense,
an interpreter.
I could call with the song
of setting stars.
I could whisper with the leaves
before rain.

It is not the cage
that prisons me.
I, who live by mimicry,
have been remade
in the image of man.

The Animals Do Judge

Indica tigris agit rabida cum tigride pacem
Perpetuam: saevis inter se convenit ursis.
Ast homini ferrum letale incude nefanda
Produxisse parum est. Juvenal

We need not wait for God
The animals do judge
Of air and sea and grass
Accusing with their eyes
Waiting here en masse
They cry out with their blood
The whale caught in surprise
By oilslick's killing sludge
The cow with poisoned milk
The elephant's muted roar
At radioactive food
The tiger's mangey hide
The silkworm's broken silk
(The animals do judge)
The dead gulls on the shore
Mists of insecticide
Killing all spore and sperm
Eagle and owl have died
and nematode and worm
The snakes drag in the mud
Fallen the lion's pride
The night moth's wings are bruised
They cry out with their blood
Cain! Killer! We are named
By beast and bird condemned
By fish and fowl accused
We need not wait for God
The animals do judge

Burn, Charity

Cold as charity, the saying goes:
I read it just now and it struck with the chill
Of the wind blowing in from the frozen river.
Cold as charity: the reluctant giver
Of love, the miser of self, cannot fill
Even himself with warmth. How the wind blows!

If I stand here in the cold I shall die
In this street of corpses and the grey near-dead.
Stone hands give out reluctant charity
And no one notices the wild disparity
Of the brilliant sun high overhead
Almost stilled by the clouds' chill cry.

My clothes keep out the heat of the sun!
I strip, I run from street to street
Chasing the distant sound of laughter,
Running, leaping, dancing after
The singing joy, my unshod feet
Glorying in the sun-warmed stone.

Naked, vulnerable, growing warm,
I meet another runner, arms spread wide
In loving and hilarious greeting.
The sun comes closer to light this meeting,
And shares our joyfulness as we stride
Laughing, exulting through wind and storm.

Nothing is everything to give,
A smile, a listening ear, a kiss,
Body and blood. Quick! Come and dine
On a crust of bread and the dregs of wine;
Never a feast was finer than this!
Come, eat and drink, unfreeze and live.

Body renewed and heart unfurled,
Love's banner blazes throughout the town
To twilight fear by law condemned,
To dayspring's joy by love redeemed.
Cold selfishness and dark be gone!
Burn, charity, and light the world!

Shout Joy!

O sing unto God
and sing praises unto his Name
magnify him that rideth upon the heavens
praise him in his Name
Jah!
shout it
cry it aloud upon the wind
take the tail of his steed
and fling across the sky
in his wild wake
Jah!
he cannot be caught
he cannot be fled
he cannot be known
nor his knowledge escaped
the light of his Name
blinds the brilliance of stars
Jah!
catch the falling dragon
ride between his flailing wings
leap between the jaws of the lion
grasp the horn of the unicorn
calling with mighty voice
Jah!
caught in star flame
whipped by comet lash
rejoice before him
cry above the voices of the cherubim
shout alongside the seraphim
Jah!

bellow joy behind kings
scattered by the quaking of his hills
fleeing before his fire
rush like snow through his thunderous flame
crying with gladness
adoration of his Name
God is Lord
Jah!

The Guests of Abraham

I saw three angels seated at the table
Radiant and calm and wise and wholly real
As we, who stumble here, are quite unable
To be or know ourselves. If they will heal
Our broken bones, heal fish and meat
And bread and wine, heal wounds of mortal flesh,
Then may we take the lower seat
And join the throng, and side by side enmesh
The ill, the whole; the old, the young; and be
A single body, breaking fallen time,
A part of this creating Trinity,
Wiser than reason, lowly, and sublime.
I saw three angels standing at my door.
Come in! Come in! as you have done before.

Jacob: Ballade

Mortal and angel wrestle through the night,
Jacob struggling, wildly wondering why
An angel should choose man for this strange fight.
The crystal ladder breaks the fragile sky
As angels watch the two throughout the dark.
At dawn the angel smites tired Jacob's thigh;
Forever will he bear the wound and mark
God's messenger has left him. And the light
Of all the watching angels rises high;
The crystal ladder breaks the fragile sky.
The world is hushed and still; the earth is stark,
Astonished at the angel's choice and Jacob's cry.
Forever will he wear the wound and mark
The Lord has left to show his humble might.
All those who wrestle thus must surely die
To live once more to show the wound's strange sight.
The crystal ladder breaks the fragile sky
As angels rise and fall. The singing lark
Herald's the wild sun's brightly rising eye.
Forever will he bear the wound and mark.

Worn Jacob limps to show that God passed by;
(The crystal ladder breaks the fragile sky
And light shines bright within the glowing dark)
Forever will he bear the wound and mark.

Moses

Come.

When?

Now. This way. I will guide you.

Wait! Not so fast.

Hurry. You. I said you.

Who am I?

Certainly I will be with thee.

Is nothing, then, what it is? I had rather the rod had
stayed a rod and not become a serpent.

Come. Quickly. While the blast of my breath opens the sea.

Stop. I'm thirsty.

Drink water from this rock.

But the rock moves on before us.

Go with it and drink.

I'm tired. Can't you stop for a while?

You have already tarried too long.

But if I am to follow you I must know your name.

I will be that I will be.

You have set the mountain on fire.

Come. Climb.

I will be lost in the terror of your cloud.

You are stiff-necked and of a stiff-necked people.

YOUR people, Lord,

Indubitably.

Your wrath waxes hot. I burn.

Thus to become great.

Show me, then, thy glory.

*No man may see my face and live. But I will cover you with
my hand while I pass by.*

My people turn away and cry because the skin of my face
shines.

Did you not expect this?
    I cannot enter the tent of the congregation while your
    cloud covers it and your glory fills the tabernacle. Look.
    It moves before us again. Can you not stay still?
Come. Follow.
    But this river is death. The waters are dark and deep.
Swim.
    Now will I see your face? Where are you taking me now?
Up the mountain with me before I die.
    But death
bursts into light.
    The death is
what it will be.
    These men: they want to keep us here in three
    tabernacles. But the cloud moves. The water springs
    from a rock that journeys on.
You are contained in me.
    But how can we contain you in ark or tabernacle or
You cannot.
    Where, then?
In your heart. Come.
    Still?
I will be with thee.
    Who am I?
You are that I will be. Come.

David

Your altar smelled of the slaughter house.
The innocent eyes of tender beasts
Lost in confusions of laws and vows
Was the high price paid to you for feasts.
They had to be men of iron, your priests.

And so did I, born but to sing,
To tend the lambs and not to kill.
Why, my Lord, did you have to bring
Me down from the safety of my hill
Into the danger of your will?

I learned to fight, I learned to sin,
I battled heathen, fought with lust;
When you were on my side I'd win.
My appetites I could not trust.
I only knew your wrath was just.

What I desired I went and stole.
I had to fight against my son.
You bound my wounds and made me whole
Despite the wrong that I had done.
I turned from you and tried to run.

You took me, also, by the hair
And brought me back before your altar.
You terrified me with your care.
Against your rage I could but falter.
You changed me, but refused to alter.

So I grew old, but there remained
Within me still the singing boy.
I stripped and sang. My wife complained.
Yet all my ill did I destroy
Dancing before you in our joy.

My God, my God, is it not meet
That I should sing and shout and roar,
Leap to your ark with loving feet?
I praise thee, hallow, and adore,
And play before thee evermore.

Song from the Fiery Furnace

Mostly I burn.
The flames change not to dew.
To ashes turn
All who lose sight of you.

O holy three
Who danced amidst the fire
Come unto me:
The furnace blazes higher.

Flames purify.
Self's idol do not mourn,
For it must die
That I to love be born.

Fire can't devour
The holy children's mirth
That turns this hour
From death to radiant birth.

O burning Son
Fiercer than furnace flame,
O purifying One,
Come, burn me with thy Name.

So, dead to sin,
Alive only in thee
My life begin
Now in eternity.

From St. Luke's Hospital (1)

To my guardian angel

Beauty and form's singular absence
Has embarrassed me before the Power
Who made all loveliness. In the hour

When the Fall's result, dark ugliness,
Shakes my body, you, Angel, come,
Solid and familiar as a nanny in the room.

Thank you, Angel, for your presence
During all the vile indignities
That accompany body's dis-ease.

You hold the beauty of the images
Which make of all creation sacrament,
Even this. Now there is no embarrassment.

Sustained by your stern confidence
In the holiness of all created things
I rest within the comfort of your wings.

From St. Luke's Hospital (2)

If I can learn a little how to die,
To die while body, mind, and spirit still
Move in their triune dance of unity,
To die while living, dying I'll fulfill
The purpose of the finite in infinity.
If God will help me learn to die today,
Today in time I'll touch eternity,
And dying, thus will live within God's Way.
If I can free myself from self's iron bands,
Freed from myself not by myself, but through
Christ's presence in this simple room, in hands
Outstretched in holy friendship, then, born new
In death, truth will outlive the deathly lie,
And in love's light I will be taught to die.

From St. Luke's Hospital (3)

Good Samaritan

She comes on at night,
older than middle-aged, from the islands,
to answer the patients' bells
to see if it's worth disturbing an overworked nurse.
At first she was suspicious, cross,
expecting complaints and impositions,
soon tender and gentle,
concerned about requests for help with pain,
coming in (without being asked)
with a blanket if it turned cold,
hoping, as she said goodbye
at the night's end, for a good day.
This morning she rushed in, frantic,
please, please could she look for the money
she had lost somehow, tending patients,
forty dollars that was not even hers.
She had kept it, in time-honored tradition,
in her bosom, and it must have fallen out
when she was thinking of someone else's needs.
She scrabbled in the wastebasket,
in the bedclothes, panted from room to room,
returned to mine with a friend. We said,
"Close the door, take off your clothes, and see
if it isn't still on you somewhere."
She did, revealing an overworked body,
wrinkled, scarred; found nothing; had to leave.
She's off now, for a week. I'll never know
if she found it or not; O God,
here, as so often, I cannot help.
Let me not forget she is your child
and your concern makes mine as nothing.

Abraham's Child

Towards afternoon the train pulled in to the station.
The light came grey and cold through the dirty glass of the
    terminal roof,
and passengers waiting on the platform blew upon their
    hands and stamped their feet
and their breath came out like smoke.
In the comfortable compartment I leaned back against the
    red plush of the seat
and looked out the window. All the signs were in a
    language I could not read.
I got out my passport and held it, waiting in readiness.
My papers were in order and the train was warm.
The conductor slid open the door to the compartment and
    said to me,
"This is your last stop on this train. You will have to get
    out."
I held out my passport, "No, no, my journey's barely half
    over,"
and I told him the cities through which the train was going
    to pass.
He handed me back my passport and said again, "You will
    have to get out,"
and he took me by the arms and led me from the coach.
His hands were so strong
    my arms cried out in pain. On the platform it was cold.
"But I don't know where I am!" I cried, "or where I am
    going."
"Follow me," he said. "I have been sent to show you."
Through the glass of the station roof I could see the sun
    was going down
and a horror of great darkness fell upon me.

"Come," the conductor said. "This is the way."
and he led me past the passengers waiting on the platform
and past the foreign signs and a burning lamp in this land
where I was a stranger. He led me to a train with no lights
and broken windows
and a pale wisp of smoke lifting from a rusty engine, and
said,
"Get in. This is your train."
I fell upon my face and laughed and said, "But this train
isn't going anywhere,"
and he said, "You may sit down," and I sat on a wooden
bench
and he put my satchel on the rack over my head.
"Are you ready for the journey?" he asked me. "I must have
your passport."
I gave it to him. "Where are we going?" I asked. The train
was cold.
"The way will be shown," he said, and closed the
compartment door.
I heard a puff of steam. The old engine began to pull the
dark car.
and we ventured out into the night.

Tree at Christmas

The children say the tree must reach the ceiling,
And so it does, angel on topmost branch,
Candy canes and golden globes and silver chains,
Trumpets that toot, and birds with feathered tails.
Each year we say, each year we fully mean:
"This is the loveliest tree of all." This tree
Bedecked with love and tinsel reaches heaven.
A pagan throwback may have brought it here
Into our room, and yet these decked-out boughs
Can represent those other trees, the one
Through which we fell in pride, when Eve forgot
That freedom is man's freedom to obey
And to adore, not to replace the light
With disobedient darkness and self-will.
On Twelfth Night when we strip the tree
And see its branches bare and winter cold
Outside the comfortable room, the tree
Is then the tree on which all darkness hanged,
Completing the betrayal that began
With that first stolen fruit. And then, O God,
This is the tree that Simon bore uphill,
This is the tree that held all love and life.
Forgive us, Lord, forgive us for that tree.
But now, still decked, adorned, in joy arrayed
For these great days of Christmas thanks and song,
This is the tree that lights our faltering way,
For when man's first and proud rebellious act
Had reached its nadir on that hill of skulls
These shining, glimmering boughs remind us that
The knowledge that we stole was freely given
And we were sent the Spirit's radiant strength

That we might know all things. We grasp for truth
And lose it till it comes to us by love.
The glory of Lebanon shines on this Christmas tree,
The tree of life that opens wide the gates.
The children say the tree must reach the ceiling,
And so it does: for me the tree has grown so high
It pierces through the vast and star-filled sky.

Annunciation

To the impossible: Yes!
Enter and penetrate
O Spirit. Come and bless
This hour: the star is late.
Only the absurdity of love
Can break the bonds of hate.

After Annunciation

This is the irrational season
When love blooms bright and wild.
Had Mary been filled with reason
There'd have been no room for the child.

Like Every Newborn

*"The Lord is King, and hath put on glorious
apparel; the Lord hath put on his apparel,
and girded himself with strength:"*

Like every newborn, he has come from very far.
His eyes are closed against the brilliance of the star.
So glorious is he, he goes to this immoderate length
To show his love for us, discarding power and strength.
Girded for war, humility his mighty dress,
He moves into the battle wholly weaponless.

The Risk of Birth, Christmas, 1973

This is no time for a child to be born,
With the earth betrayed by war & hate
And a comet slashing the sky to warn
That time runs out & the sun burns late.

That was no time for a child to be born,
In a land in the crushing grip of Rome;
Honour & truth were trampled by scorn—
Yet here did the Saviour make his home.

When is the time for love to be born?
The inn is full on the planet earth,
And by a comet the sky is torn—
Yet Love still takes the risk of birth.

The Winter Is Cold, Is Cold

The winter is cold, is cold.
All's spent in keeping warm.
Has joy been frozen, too?
I blow upon my hands
Stiff from the biting wind.
My heart beats slow, beats slow.
What has become of joy?

If joy's gone from my heart
Then it is closed to You
Who made it, gave it life.
If I protect myself
I'm hiding, Lord, from you.
How we defend ourselves
In ancient suits of mail!

Protected from the sword,
Shrinking from the wound,
We look for happiness,
Small, safety-seeking, dulled,
Selfish, exclusive, in-turned.
Elusive, evasive, peace comes
Only when it's not sought.

Help me forget the cold
That grips the grasping world.
Let me stretch out my hands
To purifying fire,
Clutching fingers uncurled.
Look! Here is the melting joy.
My heart beats once again.

Fire by Fire

My son goes down in the orchard to incinerate
Burning the day's trash, the accumulation
Of old letters, empty toilet-paper rolls, a paper plate,
Marketing lists, a discarded manuscript, on occasion
Used cartons of bird seed, dog biscuit. The fire
Rises and sinks; he stirs the ashes till the flames expire.

Burn, too, old sins, bedraggled virtues, tarnished
Dreams, remembered unrealities, the gross
Should-haves, would-haves, the unvarnished
Errors of the day, burn, burn the loss
Of intentions, recurring failures, turn
Them all to ash. Incinerate the dross. Burn. Burn.

Act III, Scene ii

Someone has altered the script.
My lines have been changed.
The other actors are shifting roles.
They don't come on when they're expected to,
and they don't say the lines I've written
and I'm being upstaged.
I thought I was writing this play
with a rather nice role for myself,
small, but juicy
and some excellent lines.
But nobody gives me my cues
and the scenery has been replaced.
I don't recognize the new sets.
This isn't the script I was writing.
I don't understand this plot at all.

To grow up
is to find
the small part you are playing
in this extraordinary drama
written by
somebody else.

The Sea Bishop

The waves, the tides, the ocean: all in tune.
Raised from the sea my pale and ancient hand
Sprays benedictions from my silver wand.
How tender now the blessing of the moon.

Raised from the sea my pale and ancient hand
Absolves all creatures of the sea and dune
(How tender now the blessing of the moon)
The birds, the shellfish, water things, and land,

Absolves all creatures of the sea and dune,
The soaring dolphin by pure moonbeams fanned,
The birds, the shellfish, water things, and land.
Across the stars the wind sweeps out its tune.
On the white whale small flecks of silver stand
Caught by the light from soaring fountain spewn.
Across the stars the wind sweeps out its tune
For all my creatures, sky, and sea, and land.

The Dragon

Please, ma'am, my references are ample.
A small group of our family has always done domestic
    service.
Look at this recommendation; just a modest sample.
I know: my distant cousins make you nervous.

But think! I can replace all those machines in your
    residence.
You call that a stove! Well, just watch *me* boil water.
May I borrow that apron, please, and the kettle? Have no
    hesitance.
Watch. I spout a little flame. Fear not, I'll never eat your
    daughter.

I haven't fancied female flesh for years.
A touch more fire. See there? The kettle's boiling.
No, I'm a vegetarian now, eat modestly, make children
    laugh, dry tears,
Need little sleep, am not afraid of toiling,

Will save you fuel on your central heating.
I'm handy at making beds and sterilizing dishes.
These dusty rugs my tail is excellent at beating.
My disposition's sweet, and I grant wishes.

On winter nights when your feet are icy cold
I make a delightfully cozy foot warmer,
Can adjust my thermostat for young or old.
If burglars come I am a superb alarmer.

I guarantee I'll give you satisfaction.
Madam, I'm hurt! Unaccustomed to such dealings!
I cannot understand your rude reaction.
Remember that a dragon, too, has feelings.

The Phoenix

*(There are many and varying legends about the beautiful
gold and scarlet bird, the Phoenix. One is that he returns
to Heliopolis every five hundred years, and that he is
born again out of his own ashes.)*

Vulnerability is my only armour.
I, the colour of fire, of blazing sun,
A blare of yellow and gold, and not a murmur
Of feathers of grey or brown, how can I run

From friend or foe? How could I ever hide?
I shall fly freely across the threatening sky
And I shall sing. Call it, if you like, pride.
I call it joy. Perhaps it's love. My eye

Is moist with all that brings it such delight.
I love this city thronging with the day,
And all the shadows crowding in the night.
Five hundred years since I have been this way,

O city full of children, wise men, fools,
Laughter and love, and hatred, scheming, murder,
Starvation among gluttons, brothels, schools;
I fly above the city and bring order

Out of this chaos. O small hungry child
Put up your bow, put down the piercing arrow
So that your hands may still be undefiled.
All through the city I must cleanse and harrow.

Aaaaagh! I am wounded by a hunter's spear.
Against the earth my dying body crashes.
The child who did not shoot me wails in fear.
Hot on my golden feathers swift blood gushes.

Blood stains the faggots of the funeral pyre.
My eyes grow dim among the flames' wild flashes.
The child is weeping still; the flames burn higher.
Hush. I shall be born from these dead ashes.

The Sea Monster

Boy! little boy!

You're going to board that ship? You dare?
To go beyond the sight of land?
They've warned you, boy? If not, beware
Of me. Beware of leaving sand

For sea. Beware of that sharp ledge
That marks the boundary of the world.
If your ship topples off the edge
I'm waiting there, my coils uncurled,

My tails athrash, my eyes afire,
My head wreathed in a flashing nimbus.
What? How dare you say that I'm a liar?
How dare you say that word: Columbus!

How dare your ship sail and not drop
When it encounters the horizon?
I wait forever for the plop
Of falling ships; I keep my eyes on

The line where sea stops at the sky,
But nothing falls: the sailing ship
Goes round and round and round and round,
A circumnavigating trip.

For land and sea are charted now;
None think of me; I am not missed.
And none can even tell you how
I talk when I do not exist.

If this round world were only square,
If this curved earth were only flat,
You'd find that I'd be waiting there,
A monster to be frightened at.

57

Instruments

Hold me against the dark: I am afraid.
Circle me with your arms. I am made
So tiny and my atoms so unstable
That at any moment I may explode. I am unable
To contain myself in unity. My outlines shiver
With the shock of living, I endeavour
To hold the *I* as one only for the cloud
Of which I am a fragment, yet to which I'm vowed
To be responsible. Its light against my face
Reveals the witness of the stars, each in its place
Singing, each compassed by the rest,
The many joined to one, the mightiest to the least.
It is so great a thing to be an infinitesimal part
Of this immeasurable orchestra the music bursts the heart,
And from this tiny plosion all the fragments join:
Joy orders the disunity until the song is one.

Body, the Black Horse and the White

Body, the black horse and the white,
Who bears me through the day and night,
How shall I ride when you are gone?
Without my steed am I undone?
Black horse and white, O winged horse,
Sinister, dextrous, holding course,
O winged horse with single horn,
O Pegasus, O unicorn,
Body my body, in the grace
Will I have any soul to save?
Body, our journey's just begun,
And rider, ridden, are only one.
How can I see your rank corruption
Except as a journey's interruption?
Where am I going? How can I travel
Without my body? Truth—unravel:
Body, as dark as starless night,
Tell me, whence comes the blinding light?
Body it is whose ears have heard
The thunder crashing of the Word.
The lightning flash reveals what face?
Where are we going? To what place?
How shall I ride when you are done?
How shall I once again be one?

Word

I, who live by words, am wordless when
I try my words in prayer. All language turns
To silence. Prayer will take my words and then
Reveal their emptiness. The stilled voice learns
To hold its peace, to listen with the heart
To silence that is joy, is adoration.
The self is shattered, all words torn apart
In this strange patterned time of contemplation
That, in time, breaks time, breaks words, breaks me,
And then, in silence, leaves me healed and mended.
I leave, returned to language, for I see
Through words, even when all words are ended.
  I, who live by words, am wordless when
  I turn me to the Word to pray. Amen.

. . . Set to the Music of the Spheres

Pain is a partner I did not request;
This is a dance I did not ask to join;
whirled in a waltz when I would stop and rest,
Jolted and jerked, I ache in bone and loin.
Pain strives to hold me close in his embrace;
If I resist and try to pull away
His grasp grows tighter; closer comes his face;
hotter his breath. If he is here to stay
Then must I learn to dance this painful dance,
Move to its rhythm, keep my lagging feet
In time with his. Thus have I a chance
To work with pain, and so may pain defeat.
Pain is my partner. If I dance with pain
Then may this wedlock be not loss but gain.

For M. S. J. 20th June, 1968

Madeleine Saunders Jones is here,
Sing joy, rejoice and celebrate!
For perfect love doth cast out fear;
All heaven laughs to mark this date,
Rejoice, rejoice,
With merry voice,
A guardian angel takes his place
To help this darling grow in grace.

Rejoice, ye people of good will
And recompense ye with this love,
This proof that wild creation still
Can pain and death by joy remove.
Take heed, take heed
This loving deed
Gives lie to darkness and to death:
Creation blows this tiny breath.

Madeleine Saunders Jones has come!
Her rosy lips move: taste and see!
She makes this groping world her home;
She curls her fingers, sucks with glee,
Is here, is here,
Beloved and dear
To all she made to watch and wait.
Rejoice! Rejoice! and celebrate!

For Dana: 4th November

The end of the year is here. We are at a new beginning.
A birth has come, and we reenact
At its remembrance the extraordinary fact
Of our unique, incomprehensible being.

The new year has started, for moving and growing.
The child's laugh within and through the adult's tears,
In joy and incomprehension at the singing years
Pushes us into fresh life, new knowing.

Here at the end of the year comes the year's springing.
The falling and melting snow meet in the stream
That flows with living waters and cleanses the dream.
The reed bends and endures and sees the dove's winging.

Move into the year and the new time's turning
Open and vulnerable and loving and steady.
The stars are aflame; creation is ready.
The day is at hand: the bright sun burns.

Charlotte Rebecca Jones, 22nd August, 1969

When the time comes it is always unexpected
And a miracle. Charlotte,
Caught in the violence of creation,
Thrust into life, disconnected
From her bearer, arrived, scarlet,
Shouting. There is no explanation

For the tearing violence of a birth.
The Lord himself, when the Word first was spoken,
Took fistfuls of formless chaos, wrested
Sky, sea, and our familiar earth
From naught. So nothingness by Love was broken
And it was good. And then God rested.

He calls his creatures each to take his part
In this great cosmic heave of love and birth,
Sharing the mighty act of his creation.
We understand this only with the heart,
With pain and joy and pure celestial mirth.
The miracle of Charlotte needs no explanation.

Charlotte

She explodes with joy.
Sparks of gold and diamond fly
from the tips of her fingers
and her dancing toes.
Her laugh is like a crystal ball
and yet it has the earthy healthiness
of blades of sun-ripe wheat.

When she implodes
with sorrow
she takes within her all the gold,
the diamonds and the sunny laughter.
Deep, deep within herself she goes
and hides the pain
protects it in her heart;
talks like an ordinary day
except the sun has gone
and the sky holds no blue.

Who knows
what thoughts she hides
from us and from herself?

She keeps her sorrow
and the scars
are underneath the flesh
unseen, enclosed within the shell.
The hidden grain of anguish
may one day turn
into a pearl.

Epithalamion:
at the time of the wedding of the first-born:

Here at the time of a newer love's beginning
I see your body suddenly anew;
Each known and tempered touch, each sense and scent,
The strong and vulnerable and infinitely dear
Feel of the flesh that clothes your living bones
Wakens my body in the old and true response
Seen once again as miracle. To see you thus
As I have always seen you, but sometimes unaware,
Is unexpected grace. There is no part
Or portion that I do not love, but now
It is the human part, the fallen flesh
That wrenches me with startling pain and joy.
These bodies that will move to death, to dust,
Made, in an act of extraordinary grace
An explosion of light, a gift of life.
Now each expression that we make of love
Makes life anew, our lives a single life,
The two made one. In tenderness and play
We light the dark, and in this joyous game
We keep alight our candle's living flame.

Crosswicks

This house has known the poignant mirth
Of two centuries of living and dying;
Is, for us, the joyful place of birth,
Has held our infant, in his cradle lying;
Has known, under the weathered roof,
The noise of our four full generations,
Weaving laughter, and tears, in its warp and woof,
Demanding forbearance, love and patience;
Saw, this spring, a wedding, love's new breath,
Promises made with sober joy; then beheld
The long weeks of my mother's dying, and her death.
Birth, love, death, our house has held,
And this epiphany affirms the worth
Of hope and prayer, this time of all Love's birth.

O Sapientia

It was from Joseph first I learned
Of love. Like me he was dismayed.
How easily he could have turned
Me from his house; but, unafraid,
He put me not away from him
(O God-sent angel, pray for him).
Thus through his love was Love obeyed.

The Child's first cry came like a bell:
God's Word aloud, God's Word in deed.
The angel spoke: so it befell,
And Joseph with me in my need.
O Child whose father came from heaven,
To you another gift was given:
Your earthly father chosen well.

With Joseph I was always warmed
And cherished. Even in the stable
I knew that I would not be harmed.
And, though above the angels swarmed,
Man's love it was that made me able
To bear God's Love, wild, formidable,
To bear God's Will, through me performed.

O Simplicitas

An angel came to me
And I was unprepared
To be what God was using.
Mother I was to be.
A moment I despaired,
Thought briefly of refusing.
The angel knew I heard.
According to God's Word
I bowed to this strange choosing.

A palace should have been
The birthplace of a king
(I had no way of knowing).
We went to Bethlehem;
It was so strange a thing.
The wind was cold, and blowing,
My coat was old, and thin.
They turned us from the inn;
The town was overflowing.

God's Word, a child so small,
Who still must learn to speak,
Lay in humiliation.
Joseph stood strong and tall.
The beasts were warm and meek
And moved with hesitation.
The Child born in a stall?
I understood it: all.
Kings came in adoration.

Perhaps it was absurd:
A stable set apart,
The sleepy cattle lowing;
And the incarnate Word
Resting against my heart.
My joy was overflowing.
The shepherds came, adored
The folly of the Lord,
Wiser than all men's knowing.

God's Beast

Least important of all animals, I am a beast
of burden. I can carry heavy loads,
and I am more patient than a camel,
gentler of nature, though occasionally stubborn.
I am not considered intelligent,
and my name is used as an insult.

But when I see an angel in my path
I recognize a messenger of God.
"Stop!" the angel said to me, and I stopped,
obeying God rather than my master, Baalam,
who hit me and cursed me and did not see
the angel's brilliance barring our way.

Later, I took the path to Bethlehem,
bearing God's bearer on my weary back,
and stood beside her in the stable, trying to share
her pain and loneliness, and then the joy.

I carried on my back the Lord himself,
riding, triumphant, through Jerusalem,
But the blessings turned to curses,
Hosanna into Crucify him! Crucify him!

Least important of all animals, beast of burden,
my heaviest burden is to turn the curse into a blessing,
to see the angel in my path,
to bear forever the blessing of my Lord.

The Tenth Hour

Who is to comfort whom
in this time beyond comfort
this end of our time?
Can I, who already have one mother,
alive, oh, very alive, and not over-willing to share,
be another man's mother's son?
Perhaps if she could hold me, as she so small a time ago
    held him,
knowing him dead with only a fragment of her knowing,
the rest of herself, her arms, heart, lips,
not understanding death—
but we will not touch. Not that way.

Can she, who has lost in such a manner her son,
be mother once again, past child-bearing, caring,
to a man full grown?
I loved her son, ran from him, returned only for the end,
most miserable—I, not he—

"Son."

My lips move. "Mother." though no sound comes.
She leaves the hill, the three crosses.
I follow. To her empty house.
She does not weep or wail as I had feared.
She does the little, homely things, prepares a meal, then
O God
washes my feet.
"An angel came," she said,
"to tell me of his birth. And I obeyed.
No angel's come to tell me of his death."

This, I thought, was not an argument.
I held back tears, since she held hers, though foolishly.
We ate—somehow—she always listening.
I said, at last, "You do not mourn."
She looked down at me gravely.
"No, my son. My second given son.
I obeyed then. Shall I do less today?"

Pentecost

Whence comes this rush of wind?
I stand at the earth's rim
And feel it streaming by
My hair, my eyes, my lips.
I shall be blown clean off.
I cannot stand the cold.

Earth shrinks. The day recedes.
The stars rush in, their fire
Blown wild as they race by.
This wind's strange, harsh embrace
Holds me against the earth,
Batters me with its power.

My bones are turned to ice.
I am not here, nor there
But caught in this great breath.
Its rhythm cracks my ribs.
Blown out, I am expelled.
Breathed in, I am inspired.

The wind broods where it will
Across the water's face.
The flowing sea of sky
Moves to the wind's demand.

The stars stretch fiery tongues
Until this mortal frame
Is seared to bone, to ash,
And yet, newborn, it lives.

Joy blazes through the night.
Wind, water, fire, are light.

Corinth

We have been further flung in time than space,
span more centuries than miles of sea,
see Apollo and his chariot race
across a long-gone sky. Here we
tread where once Medea trod,
wild and mindless, as she raged
at faithlessness of man and god,
and jealousy was not assuaged
by the wanton ruthless death
of her own sons; her mother's hand
stopped their startled, unsuspecting breath.
She stood on these stones where we stand,
before that brilliant other sun
had risen in the broken sky
when bright Apollo's race was run,
his reins relinquished with a cry.
Too far we're flung through countless years
to feel the ancient gods' swift fall
or see compassion's painful tears
groove the stern cheeks of preaching Paul.

Ready for Silence

Then hear now the silence
He comes in the silence
in silence he enters
the womb of the bearer
in silence he goes to
the realm of the shadows
redeeming and shriving
in silence he moves from
the grave cloths, the dark tomb
in silence he rises
ascends to the glory
leaving his promise
leaving his comfort
leaving his silence

So come now, Lord Jesus
Come in your silence
breaking our noising
laughter of panic
breaking this earth's time
breaking us breaking us
quickly Lord Jesus
make no long tarrying

When will you come
and how will you come
and will we be ready
for silence
            your silence

Advent, 1971

When will he come
and how will he come
and will there be warnings
and will there be thunders
and rumbles of armies
coming before him
and banners and trumpets
When will he come
and how will he come
and will we be ready

O woe to you people
you sleep through the thunder
you heed not the warnings
the fires and the drownings
the earthquakes and stormings
and ignorant armies
and dark closing on you
the song birds are falling
the sea birds are dying
no fish now are leaping
the children are choking
in air not for breathing
the aged are gasping
with no one to tend them

a bright star has blazed forth
and no one has seen it
and no one has wakened

Come, Lord Jesus!

Come, Lord Jesus! Do I dare
Cry: Lord Jesus, quickly come!
Flash the lightning in the air,
Crash the thunder on my home!
Should I speak this aweful prayer?
Come, Lord Jesus, help me dare.

Come, Lord Jesus! You I call
To come (come soon!) are not the child
Who lay once in the manger stall,
Are not the infant meek and mild.
You come in judgment on our all:
Help me to know you, whom I call.

Come, Lord Jesus! Come this night
With your purging and your power,
For the earth is dark with blight
And in sin we run and cower
Before the splendid, raging sight
Of the breaking of the night.

Come, my Lord! Our darkness end!
Break the bonds of time and space.
All the powers of evil rend
By the radiance of your face.
The laughing stars with joy attend:
Come Lord Jesus! Be my end!

Come, Let Us Gather
After A. M. Allchin's article on R. S. Thomas

Come, let us gather round the table.
Light the candles. Steward, pour the wine.
It is dark outside. The streets are noisy
with the scurrying of rats, with shoddy
tarts, shills, thugs, harsh shouting.

And what comfort is cold within? We're able
to offer a slim repast. The taste of brine,
warm from fresh tears, is in the glass. Choosy
guests will not come here. The bread is body
broken. The wine is dark with blood. I'm doubting

if half of those invited will turn up.
Most will prefer a different table,
will go elsewhere with gentler foods to sup.
And yet this is indeed a wedding feast
and we rejoice to share the bitter cup,
the crumbs of bread. For O my Lord, not least
of all that makes us raise the glass, is that we toast
You, who assembled this uncomely group: our one
      mysterious host.

At Communion

Whether I kneel or stand or sit in prayer
I am not caught in time nor held in space,
But, thrust beyond this posture, I am where
Time and eternity are face to face;
Infinity and space meet in this place
Where crossbar and upright hold the One
In agony and in all Love's embrace.
The power in helplessness which was begun
When all the brilliance of the flaming sun
Contained itself in the small confines of a child
Now comes to me in this strange action done
In mystery. Break time, break space, O wild
and lovely power. Break me: thus am I dead,
Am resurrected now in wine and bread.

Martha

Now
nobody can ever laugh at me again
I was the one who baked the bread
I pressed the grapes for wine.

Temper My Intemperance

Temper my intemperance, O Lord,
O hallowed, O adored,
My heart's creator, mighty, wild,
Temper Thy bewildered child.
Blaze my eye and blast my ear,
Let me never fear to fear
Nor forget what I have heard,
Even your voice, my Lord.
Even your Word.

Sonnet after Thomas

Thomas doubted: seeing, then believed;
Touched the wounded hands, the pierced side,
Knew once for all his Lord and God; received
The Word and taught it. While I, Lord, in my pride
Am shown your light and still trip over doubt,
Seeking in foolishness to understand
The infinite with my finite wit, am out,
Then, of my mortal mind; reject your hand
At the same moment that I hold it tight.
Knowing, I know not all the things I know;
Hearing, I hear not; seeing, seek the light;
Standing, fly skywards; running, am too slow.
    Here in captivity where my song is wrung
    Help me to find again my native tongue.

Love Letter

I hate you, God.
Love, Madeleine.

> I write my message on water
> and at bedtime I tiptoe upstairs
> and let it flow under your door.

When I am angry with you
I know that you are there
even if you do not answer my knock
even when your butler opens the door an inch
and flaps his thousand wings in annoyance
at such untoward interruption
and says that the master is not at home.

> I love you, Madeleine.
> Hate, God.

(This is how I treat my friends, he said to one great saint.
No wonder you have so few of them, Lord, she replied.)

> I cannot turn the other cheek
> It takes all the strength I have
> To keep my fist from hitting back
> the soldiers shot the baby
> the little boys trample the old woman
> the gutters are filled with groans
> while pleasure seekers knock each other down
> in order to get their tickets stamped first.

I'm turning in my ticket
and my letter of introduction.
You're supposed to do the knocking. Why do you burst
    my heart?

        How can I write you
        to tell you that I'm angry
        when I've been given the wrong address
        and I don't even know your real name?

I take hammer and nails
and tack my message on two crossed pieces of wood:

        Dear God
        is it too much to ask you
        to bother to be?
        Just show your hindquarters
        and let me hear you roar.

Love,
Madeleine

For Ascension Day, 1967

I know it's not like that sunny Sunday afternoon
When we went to the zoo; evening came too soon
And we were back on the crowded city street
Still full of pleasure from the afternoon's treat,
And our little girl clutched in her fingers a blue balloon.

It bobbed above our heads. Suddenly there came a cry,
A howl of absolute loss. We looked on high
And there we saw the balloon, ascending,
Turning and twirling higher and higher, blending
Into the smoky blue of the city sky.

We wiped the eyes, blew the little nose, consoled the tears,
Did not, of course, offer a new balloon, instead were silly,
    waggled our ears,
Turned sobs to laughter, accepted loss, and hurried
Home for dinner. This day is not like that. And yet they
    must have tarried,
Looking up into the sky the day he left them, full of loss
    and fears.

He had come back to them, was with them, and then was
    lost
Again, or so perhaps it seemed, the table left without the
    host.
The disciples did not understand all that he had said,
That comfort would be sent; there would be wine and
    bread.
Lost and abandoned (where is my blue balloon?) they did
    not comprehend until the day of Pentecost.

Even after he told them, his followers did not hear and see:
What is this that he saith unto us? A little while and ye
Shall not see me, and again a little while and ye shall . . . .
    when? tomorrow?
We do not understand. Lord, nor do I, and share thus in
    their sorrow.
At the same time that the Spirit sets my sorrow free
To turn to love, and teaches me through pain to know
That love will dwell in me, and I in love, only if I let
    love go.

After the Saturday Liturgy at Montfort

O taste, and see, how gracious the Lord is:
taste! and see
    bread, fresh and hot from the oven,
    spring water, bubbling up from the rocks on a hot day,
    tears, salt and warm as I kiss away a child's hurt,
    wine, shared, as the cup is passed,
    tears, salt and bitter, my tears, hot with pain,
    lips, tender and loving, comforting and healing,
O taste! taste and see.

O hear, and see, how gracious the Lord is:
hear! hear and see
    the thunder of his joy as galaxies fling across the Cosmos,
    the whisper of grass growing,
    the voice of the beloved,
    my own fingers finding the sound of Bach.
    the greeting of friends,
    laughter and sharing and song,
    and the words of healing bringing new life.
O hear! hear and see.

O sniff, smell and see, how gracious the Lord is:
smell! sniff and see
    the salt of the ocean and the rush of wind,
    the sweet puckering smell of grapes being pressed for
      wine,
    the odour of rising dough, promise of bread,
    and oh, did you know you can recognize your own baby
      by its smell?
    and those you love most dearly, too, the unique, original
      smell of flesh

created—like flaming suns, like the smallest hydrogen
    atom—
to the honour and glory of his Name
O sniff! smell and see.

O feel, and see, how gracious the Lord is:
Feel! touch and see
    bread in your fingers; feel it, bite and swallow;
    and wine, warm and living, spreading its fire through
        your body;
    take my hand, let me take yours, touch,
    so moves the Spirit through us—O touch me, heal me,
        hold me—
    God moves through our fingers—
    Reach out, touch the sun
    do not be afraid, O swallower of flame
    for this fire burns in order to give life.

Feel! Touch and see
        how gracious the Lord is!
Taste, hear, smell, feel and see
        how gracious the Lord is!

Star Light

Perhaps
　　after death
the strange timelessness, matterlessness,
　　absolute differentness
　　　　of eternity
will be shot through
like a starry night
with islands of familiar and beautiful
joys.

For I should like
to spend a star
sitting beside Grandpapa Bach
at the organ, learning, at last, to play
　　the C minor fugue as he, essentially,
　　heard it burst into creation;

and another star
　　of moor and mist, and through the shadows
　　the cold muzzle of the dog against my hand,
　　and walk with Emily. We would not need to
　　talk, nor ever go back to the damp of
　　Haworth parsonage for tea.

I should like to eat a golden meal
　　with my brothers Gregory and Basil,
　　and my sister Macrina. We would raise
　　our voices and laugh and be a little drunk
　　with love and joy.

I should like a theatre star,
    and Will yelling, "No! No! that's not
    how I wrote it! but perhaps it's better
    that way: 'To be or not to be:' All
    right, then! Let it stand!"

And I should like
    another table
    —Yes, Plato, please come, and you, too,
    Socrates, for this is the essential table
    of which all other tables are only
    flickering shadows on the wall.
    This is the heavenly banquet,
    (Oh, come!)
    the eternal convivium.

The sky blazes with stars!

Ascension, 1969

Pride is heavy.
It weighs.
It is a fatness of spirit,
an overindulgence in self.
This gluttony is earthbound
Cannot be lifted up.
Help me to fast,
to lost this weight!
Otherwise, O Light One,
how can I rejoice in your
Ascension?

Confession Shortly Before
the Forty-eighth Birthday

Here I am, beyond the middle middle,
According to chronology,
No closer to solving cosmic or private riddle,
No further from apology
For clumsy self's continuing ineptitude,
Still shaken by the heart's wild battering.
Intemperate passions constantly intrude;
I cannot keep small hurts from mattering,
Am shattered when met with mild irritation,
Need reassurance, feel inadequate and foolish,
Seek love's return, bump into abrogation,
Am stubborn beyond the point of being merely mulish.
So am I saved only by the strange stern power of silence,
The disciplined joy of work and rule
Inner and outer imposed, steel cold. The violence
Of the freezing wind sustains the heart. So this poor fool
Is fed, is nourished, forgets then to be concerned with rust;
Repentance, too, is turning, if towards dust,
And gratitude sings forth in adoration
Of the one who touched and healed the halt and lame
With the aweful, blissful power of his spoken Name.

Testament

O God
I will do thy will.
I will
to do thy will.

How can my will
will to do thy will?
If I will
to know thy will
then I fall on my own will.
How can I will
to love or to obey?
My very willing bars the way.
Willingness becomes self-will.

O God
if thou will
turn my will to thy will
if thou will
tell me thy will
it will
be in spite of
not because of
my will.

Help me to lose my will.
Each day
let my will die
so will I
be born.
New born will I live
willingly
lovingly
and will
will be no more
will be thine
O God
if thou will.

Sonnet, Trinity 18

Peace is the centre of the atom, the core
Of quiet within the storm. It is not
A cessation, a nothingness; more
The lightning in reverse is what
Reveals the light. It is the law that binds
The atom's structure, ordering the dance
Of proton and electron, and that finds
Within the midst of flame and wind, the glance
In the still eye of the vast hurricane.
Peace is not placidity: peace is
The power to endure the megatron of pain
With joy, the silent thunder of release,
The ordering of Love. Peace is the atom's start,
The primal image: God within the heart.